CONTENTS

U.S. ASSISTANCE TO SOUTH ASIA: IS THERE A STRATEGY TO GO WITH ALL THAT MONEY?

WEDNESDAY, MAY 14, 2008,

HOUSE OF REPRESENTATIVES,
SUBCOMMITTEE ON THE MIDDLE EAST
AND SOUTH ASIA,
COMMITTEE ON FOREIGN AFFAIRS,
Washington, DC.

The subcommittee met, pursuant to notice, at 2 o'clock p.m. in room 2172, Rayburn House Office Building, Hon. Gary L. Ackerman (chairman of the subcommittee) presiding.

Mr. ACKERMAN. The subcommittee will come to order. Last week I suggested that the major elements of U.S. foreign assistance consisted, metaphorically speaking, of sending lawyers, guns and money, that promoting democracy, free markets, civil society and the rule of law strengthens our partners in the international community, that supporting our allies with appropriate arms and training is morally and smart policy and that using our wealth and access to our economy to friendly nations to grow their economies and develop their governance capacity is a smart use of our taxpayers' money.

In essence, lawyers, guns and money are the key pillars supporting American foreign policy. Each element has its limit as well. In South Asia, all three components are necessary but are not by themselves sufficient. Pillars are just that, pillars. They are not the whole structure. They are tools and tactics to help us achieve our policy goals. In South Asia, they are often tactics in search of a strategy.

South Asia is arguably the place from which America faces the greatest terrorist threat. It was in Afghanistan that al-Qaeda plotted and carried out the attacks of September 11.

It is in the tribal areas of Pakistan where al-Qaeda and the Taliban have reconstituted themselves and from where they attack our forces as well as those of both Afghanistan and Pakistan, yet, since the beginning of the year there has been a series of reports all of which suggest the United States has no overall strategy for dealing with Afghanistan, Pakistan or the terrorist threat that emanates from both.

With regard to Afghanistan, the Atlantic Council states: Make no mistake, NATO is not winning in Afghanistan. The Center for the Study of the Presidency's Afghanistan Study Group concludes: The mission to stabilize Afghanistan is faltering. The International Crisis Group maintains: Afghanistan is not lost but the signs are not good.

In the case of Pakistan, the Government Accountability Office found that: The United States has not met its national security goals to destroy the terrorist threat and close the safe haven in Pakistan's FATA region. While the President and his administration don't seem very adept when it comes to strategy, either of having one or implementing one, the Bush administration is very good at spending money, lots of it, and mostly on guns.

In terms of foreign assistance and even in terms of United States policy, South Asia was a backwater until September 2001. From that point forward, U.S. assistance and attention to the region skyrocketed. Since America was attacked, South Asia has become second only to the Middle East in terms of United States military assistance.

Over the past 6 years the United States has spent $15.6 billion on training for the Afghan National Army and police, yet, that army is still incapable of operating on its own, and the police are so bad that most Afghans are more afraid of them than they are of the Taliban.

In Pakistan over the same 6-year period, the Bush administration has provided $1.6 billion in foreign military financing and $5.56 billion in coalition support funds.

The former funds to buy radars and antisubmarine planes to track the nonexistent al-Qaeda Air Force and Navy, and the latter funds disappeared into the Pakistani treasury for unspecified services allegedly rendered, yet, Pakistani officials complain, and have done so to me directly, that they lack the capabilities and training to conduct effective counterinsurgency operations.

So we shouldn't be too surprised that the GAO supports the claim that found that "Pakistani security forces lack counterinsurgency capability," that the Pakistani Army is "neither structured nor trained for counterinsurgency," and that serious equipment and training deficiencies exist in the frontier course. What did the Bush administration spend all that money on?

If the situation weren't so dire and our need for resources not so absolute, I would suggest that additional appropriations to security forces in either nation was throwing good money after bad.

Leaving the urgent to address the merely very important for a moment, there are other nations in South Asia which are in various stages of civil war reconciliation or government transition where the right mix of lawyers, guns and money could mean the difference between a failed state and democratic development.

In Sri Lanka, the government continues to prosecute the war against the LTTE, the Tamil Terrorist Group, but in provincial actions on Saturday, a splinter group of the LTTE gained enough seats in a coalition with the ruling party to form the next provincial government. Press reports, however, indicate that the election was fraught with irregularities, such as ballot box stuffing, voter intimidation and beatings.

Because former LTTE members who face accusations of murder, harassing opposition voters and candidates and recruiting child soldiers will now be part of the provincial government, the Bush administration is faced with the legal question of how to provide assistance to the areas of the country partially controlled by an organization which while not actually designated a foreign terrorist organization used to be part of one.

In Nepal, the Maoists did surprisingly well in elections for the constituent assembly, so well, in fact, that they will now not only be writing a new constitution but will likely be forming a new government. Since the Maoists are a designated foreign terrorist organization the continued provision of United States assistance to Nepal appears on its face to be illegal.

While no one supports funding terrorist organizations, continued reconciliation and democratic development in Nepal is in the interest of the United States, so I, for one, will be interested to hear whether the administration believes that assistance to Nepal should continue, and, if so, how it intends to proceed.

In Bangladesh, the caretaker government, which has lasted a lot longer than a caretaker government ought, is preparing for elections hopefully by the end of this year. I support the administration's call for lifting emergency rule. Free, fair and transparent elections cannot be conducted when the rights to speak and assemble are restricted.

The caretaker government has taken a partial step allowing in door political gatherings, but it must go much further to ensure a legitimate election in December. The one country I haven't spoken about is India, a giant sea of relative tranquility surrounded by chaos and instability. India has experienced enormous economic growth in recent years, but it still has .75 billion people who live on less than $1 a day.

In another context, that is almost as many people as in Canada, the United States, Mexico, Central and all of South America combined. Three-quarters of a billion people who live on less than $1 a day and face serious public health problems, such as the threat of HIV/AIDS and the lack of potable water. Even though India is a growing stronger economy, I am still dismayed that the administration chose to cut funding for HIV/AIDS.

While I don't think that countries should receive our assistance indefinitely, I do think we run the risk of undoing processes already made by cutting assistance prematurely. Lawyers, guns and money. Each one is essential but in different degrees in different countries. Each is insufficient by itself.

Without a strategy to bind them together they are only means without an end. Unfortunately, that is what we have seen from the administration in this region. Since 2001, we have spent $38.67 billion and we are no closer to a peaceful, stable, secure South Asia than when we began. As I said last week, that is quite a legacy.

Now, I will turn to the ranking member, my partner in conducting this hearing, the Honorable Michael Pence.

[The prepared statement of Mr. Ackerman follows:]

PREPARED STATEMENT OF THE HONORABLE GARY L. ACKERMAN, A REPRESENTATIVE IN CONGRESS FROM THE STATE OF NEW YORK, AND CHAIRMAN, SUBCOMMITTEE ON THE MIDDLE EAST AND SOUTH ASIA

Good afternoon. The subcommittee will come to order. Last week I suggested that the major elements of U.S. foreign assistance consisted, metaphorically speaking, of sending Lawyers, Guns and Money: that promoting democracy, free markets, civil society, and the rule of law strengthens our partners in the international community; that supporting our allies with appropriate arms and training is morally right and smart policy; and that using our wealth and access to our economy to help friendly nations to grow their economies and to develop their governance capacity is a smart use of our taxpayers' money. In essence, Lawyers, Guns and Money are the key pillars supporting American foreign policy, but each element has its limit as well. In South Asia, all three components are necessary but are not, by themselves, sufficient. Pillars are are just that, pillars. They are not the whole structure; they are tools and tactics to help us achieve our policy goals. And in South Asia, they are often tactics in search of a strategy.

South Asia is arguably the place from which America faces the greatest terrorist threat. It was in Afghanistan that al Qaeda plotted and carried out the attacks of September 11. It is in the tribal areas of Pakistan where al Qaeda and the Taliban have reconstituted themselves and from where they attack our forces, as well as those of both Afghanistan and Pakistan. Yet since the beginning of the year there has been a series of reports all of which suggest the United States has no overall strategy for dealing with Afghanistan, Pakistan or the terrorist threat the emanates from both.

With regard to Afghanistan, the Atlantic Council states: "Make no mistake, NATO is not winning in Afghanistan." The Center for the Presidency's Afghanistan Study Group concludes: "The mission to stabilize Afghanistan is faltering." The International Crisis Group maintains: "Afghanistan is not lost but the signs are not good."

In the case of Pakistan, the Government Accountability Office found that, "The United States has not met its national security goals to destroy the terrorist threat and close the safe haven in Pakistan's FATA region."

While the President and his Administration don't seem very adept when it comes to strategy, either having one or implementing one, the Bush Administration is very good at spending money, lots of it and mostly on guns. In terms of foreign assistance, and even in terms of U.S. policy, South Asia was a backwater until September 2001. From that point forward, U.S. assistance and attention to the region sky-rocketed. Since America was attacked, South Asia has become second only to the Middle East in terms of U.S. military assistance. Over the past 6 years, the United States has spent $15.6 Billion on training for the Afghan National Army and Police, yet the army is still incapable of operating on its own and the police are so bad that most Afghans are more afraid of them than they are of the Taliban.

In Pakistan, over the same six year period, the Bush Administration has provided $1.5 Billion in Foreign Military Financing and $5.56 Billion in Coalition Support Funds. The former to buy radars, and anti submarine planes to track the non-existent al Qaeda air force and navy and the latter disappeared into the Pakistani Treasury for unspecified services allegedly rendered. Yet Pakistani officials complain, and have done so to me directly, that they lack the capabilities and training to conduct effective counter-insurgency operations. So we shouldn't be too surprised that the GAO supports that claim and found that: "Pakistani security forces lack counterinsurgency capability"; that the Pakistani Army "is neither structured nor trained for counterinsurgency"; and that "serious equipment and training deficiencies exist in the Frontier Corps." What did the Bush Administration spend all that money on? If the situation weren't so dire and our need for success not so absolute, I'd suggest that additional appropriations to security forces in either nation was throwing good money after bad.

Leaving the urgent to address the merely important for a moment, there are other nations in South Asia which are in various stages of civil war reconciliation, or governmental transition where the right mix of Lawyers, Guns and Money could mean the difference between a failed state and democratic development. In Sri Lanka, the government continues to prosecute the war against the LTTE, the Tamil terrorist group, but in provincial elections on Saturday, a splinter group of the LTTE gained enough seats in a coalition with the ruling party to form the next provincial government. Press reports, however, indicate that the election was fraught with irregularities like ballot-box stuffing, voter intimidation and beatings. Because former LTTE members, who face accusations of murder, harassing opposition voters and candidates and recruiting child soldiers, will now be part of the provincial government, the Bush Administration is faced with the legal question of how to provide assistance to areas of the country partially controlled by an organization, which while not actually designated a foreign terrorist organization used to be part of one.

In Nepal, the Maoists did surprisingly well in elections for the constituent assembly. So well, in fact, that they will now not only be writing a new constitution but will likely be forming a new government. Since the Maoists are a designated Foreign Terrorist Organization, the continued provision of U.S. assistance to Nepal appears on its face to be illegal. While no one supports funding terrorist organizations, continued reconciliation and democratic development in Nepal is in the interest of the United States, so I will be interested to hear whether the Administration believes assistance to Nepal should continue and if so, how it intends to proceed.

In Bangladesh, the caretaker government, which has lasted a lot longer than a caretaker government ought to, is preparing for elections, hopefully by the end of this year. I support the Administration's call for lifting emergency rule. Free, fair and transparent elections cannot be conducted when the rights to speak and assemble are restricted. The caretaker government has taken a partial step, allowing indoor political gatherings, but it must go much further to ensure a legitimate election in December.

The one country I haven't spoken about is India, a giant sea of relative tranquility surrounded by chaos and instability. India has experienced enormous economic growth in recent years, but it still has three-quarters of a billion people who live on less than a dollar a day and faces serious public health problems like the threat of HIV/AIDS and a lack of potable water. And even though India is growing stronger economically, I am still dismayed that the Administration chose to cut funding for HIV/AIDS. While I don't think that countries should receive our assistance indefinitely, I do think we run the risk of undoing progress already made by cutting assistance prematurely.

Lawyers, Guns and Money. Each one is necessary but in different degrees in different countries; each is insufficient by itself. Without a strategy to bind them together they are only means without an end. And that unfortunately, is what we have seen from the Bush Administration in this region. Since 2001 we've spent $38.67 Billion and we are no closer than we were when we began to a peaceful, stable, secure South Asia. As I said last week, that's some legacy.

Mr. PENCE. Thank you, Mr. Chairman. Mr. Chairman, we had grim reminders this week. Enormous natural disasters coupled with government malfeasance and even malevolence in Asia in the last 2 weeks in China and in Burma have reminded us that the world is always with us and in this general area are ever with us whether we want it to be or not.

The region of South Asia specifically is sometimes overlooked, not by our esteemed witnesses today, who through the course of their professional lives and their present service do great credit to themselves and to the United States of America, and I welcome them. I also want to say the region of South Asia, while overlooked by some, is never overlooked by this subcommittee. I am grateful for the chairman's leadership in calling this important hearing

The threat of Islamic terrorism looms large in this region, notably in the front lines of the war on terror in Afghanistan and Pakistan. This is not the extent of dangerous and destabilizing forces, I would argue. There are Maoist insurgents in Nepal, Tamil Tigers in Sri Lanka, and some of these forces have even had unwelcome electoral success in recent days.

Mr. Chairman, on the subject of aid, linking means and ends is a vital undertaking. Those of us with some responsibility for U.S. foreign policy recognize that. Foreign assistance cannot be viewed in isolation of our foreign policy. I make no apology for the idea that our scarce taxpayer resources must be directed to our national interest.

As I said in our hearing last week, it is my judgment foreign assistance must not be viewed as charity, it must be driven by our national interest.

Clearly in the 47-year history of the Foreign Assistance Act of 1961, Congress and several administrations have merely added programs so that over time it now includes more than 33 major objectives, 75 priorities, 247 directives, none of which, according to Congressional Research Services' report to us, "are prioritized, making it less effective in demonstrating a coordinated foreign aid strategy."

This dizzying array of programs is probably not optimally arranged. So as the chairman asks is there a strategy to go with the money, the President's U.S. National Security Strategy of 2002 and then 2006 identify global development as a pillar. Ambassador Boucher makes it clear what this means saying, "promoting democratic stability as the base from which to counter extremism and terrorism."

Mr. Ward also echoes this stating USAID's goals as "strengthening local governments' abilities to provide basic human services and economic opportunity." These goals are laudable, but it is a legitimate question if we are maximizing our strength and the use of soft power. I am pleased to have this committee raise these issues today.

In light of that, I would question some of our short-sighted trade policies. I think the absurdity of our trade barriers is highlighted by one of our committee's witness testimony last month who said, "we give $80 million in foreign assistance to Bangladesh, but we charge it $500 million in tariffs." This is a classic case of the left hand not knowing what the right hand is doing in American foreign affairs.

Now, surely, trade, not aid, is an approach we can offer to some of those growing economies in South Asia. I am particularly intrigued about Ambassador Boucher's background and Mr. Ward. Both of your testimonies mentioned reconstruction opportunity zones in Afghanistan. While I may be pulled off to the floor, I will be reviewing your testimony carefully.

I would be very curious what our witnesses have to say about the possibility of pursuing a bipartisan free trade agreement with Afghanistan, a subject about which this member and some other members have begun some preliminary conversations. It is hard for me to imagine Afghanistan's burgeoning economy as a threat to American economic interests, but I would welcome response to that.

On a positive note, I want to laud the work of USAID in provincial reconstruction themes in Afghanistan. I observed a bridge project underway in Kunar province in March of this year on Codel Costa. Mr. Ward's testimony highlights that some USAID personnel are embedded with United States Special Forces in reaching some of the most dangerous areas of Afghanistan, and I saw it firsthand.

I have to tell you, the thumbs up that I got from the Afghan citizens who were working on that bridge project down there breaking rocks but proudly wearing blue jerseys was deeply humbling to me, and, in addition to the soldiers that were in our company, it made me terribly proud to be an American to see the pride on their faces. So I commend you all for your leadership in that regard. It is truly noble.

I believe it is also a wise approach to leveraging interagency efforts in this regard between Special Forces and USAID, and I hope to see that continue. Mr. Chairman, thank you again for calling this hearing. Thank you for the challenging issues raised by it. I yield back.

Mr. ACKERMAN. Thank you very much. There being no other members that requested time to speak, we now turn to our very distinguished witnesses. Assistant Secretary of State Richard Boucher, a career Foreign Service Officer, has provided distinguished service to our nation for 30 years. He was sworn in as the Assistant Secretary of State for South and Central Asian Affairs on February 21, 2006.

Over the course of his career, Ambassador Boucher has served as the State Department spokesman or deputy spokesman under six Secretaries of State and has served as Chief of Mission twice overseas. Ambassador Boucher's early career focused on economic affairs, China and Europe. Ambassador Boucher, welcome back to the subcommittee.

We will also hear from Mr. Mark Ward, Senior Deputy Assistant Administrator for USAID's Bureau for Asia. Mr. Ward has served our nation with distinction for 20 years and has chaired USAID's Lebanon Reconstruction Task Force, as well as having previously led USAID's task force efforts in 2005 to respond to the Southeast Asian tsunami and the South Asian earthquake.

Mr. Ward is a career minister in the Senior Foreign Service and has served in Pakistan, Egypt, the Philippines, as well as Russia. Mr. Ward, welcome back to the subcommittee to you as well. Without objection, each of your complete statements will be made part of the record.

Ambassador Boucher, we will begin with you. We are making technical adjustments, like plugging something in. We have our own local reconstruction project going on. We have a whole room filled with electronic equipment over there and the guy who knows how to run it who is over there. We have now reunited the technician and the technology.

[Pause.]

Mr. ACKERMAN. I am back. The chair will ask our witnesses if they would relocate themselves on the first level and take the members' microphones. If the staff can operate both sets of cameras so that—we don't know who operates the cameras. There is somebody hidden somewhere. If the people who know how to work the cameras are somewhere near the cameras—those aren't working either?

Well, come up one more level. You are now in purgatory. You are ascending rapidly.

Mr. WARD. Hello? That one is working.

Mr. ACKERMAN. All right.

Mr. WARD. We have got a working one here.

Mr. ACKERMAN. Okay. We have working microphones here.

Mr. BOUCHER. Hello? Mr. Chairman. Thank you.

Mr. ACKERMAN. You can both be seated. If you prefer not to stand, we forgive your back, and if the camera people can accommodate us somehow we will be able to get a frontal view on the screen and the audience can see all of us. Now, for the first time, the audience can see the witnesses live. Ambassador Boucher, you are not used to live audiences, I know. People usually saw you on that little screen.

STATEMENT OF THE HONORABLE RICHARD A. BOUCHER, ASSISTANT SECRETARY, BUREAU OF SOUTH AND CENTRAL ASIAN AFFAIRS, U.S. DEPARTMENT OF STATE

Mr. BOUCHER. Mr. Chairman, thank you. I have to say, this is a very unique experience.

Mr. ACKERMAN. Welcome to the committee. We will not call for any votes.

Mr. BOUCHER. I can see why you like it up here. Mr. Chairman, if I can, I would like to begin by expressing a sentiment that I think you share, Mr. Pence, and the other members of the committee, and that is absolute condemnation of the terrorist attacks in Jaipur yesterday in India.

It is a sad reminder that even as, I think you called it the glowing light in the region, the more stable country that is developing, is still subject to these horrible kinds of attacks and we need to work with the people of India as we express our sympathy. We all know there is no justification for the murders of innocent people in that way, and we need to work with the Indians to try to help them prevent such attacks in the future.

I want to thank you as well for hosting this hearing today. South and Central Asia I think is a region that we all agree involves vital interest for the United States. There are millions and millions of people there, especially young people, who want opportunity in their lives but who are also pressed——

[Electronic interference.]

Mr. BOUCHER [continuing]. I think we are back, yes. It is a region that faces enormous challenges from terrorists and insurgencies to melting glaciers and floods. We think the United States is uniquely capable and uniquely positioned to help people in this region and that by doing so we make people at home safer. It will require from us a long-term effort. Problems we are dealing with were decades in the making, and solutions will take time.

We do have a consistent policy basis in the region, that is, to promote democratic stability is the best base to counter extremism. To accomplish those goals we do several things. First, we support efforts to build democracy.

Things like, for example, the way we work to improve governments, especially at local levels in Afghanistan, or how we have been pressing and supporting strengthened institutions into judiciary in Pakistan and Bangladesh. Second, we support what I call the foundations of democracy: Education, technology, rule of law, information.

Education, for example, we are looking for new opportunities in India supporting expansion of the modern education system in Pakistan as a way to give kids a modern education that prepares them for society instead of having them be drawn in to radical madrassahs.

Furthermore, throughout the region we try to support access to information, to technology, so that people can join the modern world and participate in modern world affairs. Third, we support the opportunities that people are looking for for themselves and for their children.

We have strong economic support programs everywhere from Sri Lanka to Kazakhstan, which is, I know, not in your committee, but it is in my region at top end. We support healthcare for needy populations in Bangladesh and in India, especially when it comes to combating HIV/AIDS.

We are building infrastructure that is needed for private sector growth in the region, especially in Afghanistan, where the key components of many of our programs are roads, electricity, irrigation systems; the capabilities that people need to develop their own lives and their own economies.

A fourth big area is we support the security services in their fight against terrorism, so we spend a lot of money, as you correctly noted, building the Afghan Army and police force, which is a key element in stabilizing the country. We are embarked on a program now to help transform the Pakistani security forces in the tribal areas so that they are better able to provide security for the people who live in those areas.

We are providing antiterrorism assistance and courses in Bangladesh, Pakistan and other places, and we have border control and narcotics programs in Afghanistan and in all its neighbors. Our assistance budgets reflect these priorities: $331 million for democracy this year, $503 million——

[Electronic interference.]

Mr. BOUCHER [continuing]. $366 million for economic programs and $791 million for security and counternarcotics programs.

In addition to the programs we have been running for a while and expanding and moving in to for a while, we see new opportunities and new challenges to deal with, challenges in Afghanistan that require a special effort on governance and security issues.

The government in Afghanistan is indeed taking initiatives in the districts and the provinces, and we need to do what we can to provide a consistent stream of money to help governors and others carry out provincial development plans and local projects that meet the needs of the population.

The new government in Pakistan, the successful transition to a democratic government in Pakistan that we worked so hard on last year is now in a position to set its own priorities and to work to develop its own country in the way that they were elected to do.

So we are talking to the new government about how we can help them modernize education, modernize the economy, modernize democratic institutions and modernize their security forces in order to develop the country, meet peoples' needs, and, above all, counter extremism in the society. Again and again as I travel throughout this region I find that people look to the United States for help.

We are being asked right now to mobilize efforts to deal with the food crisis and the energy problems. We are being asked for assistance and support for national goals that governments, including democratic governments, are setting. The United States' public sector and the private sector in the end can provide what ordinary people want for their children: Safe environment, education, technology, opportunities for jobs based on merit and not who you were born to.

In turn, the United States benefits from any stability that we create in this region. It protects us and it opens up opportunities for us as well. So my conclusion is that we need to continue to engage consistently and strategically in this vital region on the basis that I said, building democratic stability to fight extremism, and that we need to find new and interesting ways to do that year, after year, after year.

So with those remarks, sir, I would be glad to take your questions. I won't try to go into all the things you mentioned in your opening remarks, but I am happy to deal with them if you want to raise them.

Mr. ACKERMAN. Thank you very much. Mr. Ward.

[The prepared statement of Mr. Boucher follows:]

PREPARED STATEMENT OF THE HONORABLE RICHARD A. BOUCHER, ASSISTANT SECRETARY, BUREAU OF SOUTH AND CENTRAL ASIAN AFFAIRS, U.S. DEPARTMENT OF STATE

Chairman Ackerman, thank you for the opportunity to address you and the Subcommittee today on the President's Fiscal Year 2009 request for assistance to the countries of South Asia.

I'm pleased to be testifying today with Mark Ward, the Senior Deputy Assistant Administrator for Asia at the U.S. Agency for International Development. Our two Bureaus are absolute partners in the planning and delivery of foreign assistance in the region, so I suspect we'll be repeating each other a bit today.

As you know, Mr. Chairman, September 11, 2001 cast a spotlight on South and Central Asia for the United States and many other countries around the world. Our engagement there suddenly became more critical to our national security than perhaps anywhere else. In my opinion, that remains true today.

South Asia is a part of the world where we see extremely difficult challenges: poverty, disease, terrorism, drugs, weak governance, corruption and natural disasters to name some of them. We also have great opportunities, with a population of over a billion people, most of them young and increasingly connected to each other and the rest of the world. The capabilities, resources and ideals of the United States uniquely position us to help transform the region into one rooted in democratic stability and committed to fighting extremism.

While the needs are near infinite, fiscal realities dictate that we, as policy makers, think strategically, allocate strategically and work with other countries to ensure that we pursue those things that contribute most to the safety, stability and prosperity of the people of the region.

THE STRATEGIC VISION

The United States has a consistent policy basis throughout the region: promoting democratic stability as the base from which to counter extremism and terrorism. We do this by supporting efforts to build democratic institutions. We do this by supporting the foundations of democracy: education, rule of law, access to information, technology. We do this by supporting the opportunities all people want, in education, health care and the economy. And, we do this by supporting those institutions that provide security, fight terror and fight drugs.

While these efforts manifest themselves in different ways through different programs in different countries, what we pursue is not haphazard and it is not coincidence. It's considered strategic policy. And, in South Asia, we're pursuing it with the most important things we have: democratic ideals, money and manpower.

SUPPORTING EFFORTS TO BUILD DEMOCRATIC INSTITUTIONS

All of the countries in South Asia are working towards becoming stable democracies, but the great majority of them have not yet arrived. Across the region, our assistance is geared towards increasing the capacity of governments to deliver basic services, security, rule of law, and economic opportunity in a manner that respects human rights and reflects the principles of democratic, good governance. When governments deliver in a transparent and effective manner, the space for extremists and insurgents to operate with impunity closes.

Promoting good governance and institutions figures prominently in our budgets in Afghanistan, where we are working with a particular focus at the local and district level. Our efforts are closely coordinated with the Afghan Government, who took the initiative this past summer to actively improve its ability to provide for its people with the establishment of the Independent Directorate for Local Governance. Money requested in the 2009 base budget will bolster this Afghan initiative by supporting this office's ability to empower local officials and enhance their ability to serve their people.

In addition to tying people to their government through the provision of vital services, citizens must also be able to choose their government in free and fair elections. In Afghanistan, we attach great importance to the upcoming presidential and parliamentary elections as an essential part of the transition to a full democracy. Our Fiscal Year 2008 supplemental and 2009 budget requests include $193 million for upcoming presidential, parliamentary, and provincial elections with an additional $113 million in 2009 supplemental bridge funding for municipal and district-level elections.

We've also worked very closely with Pakistan and are focusing our assistance on helping the country make a smooth transition to elected government. The recent election outcome in Pakistan illustrated the Pakistani people's commitment to democracy. Their choosing of a government comprised of moderate political parties also demonstrates a desire to reject violent extremists. The United States must help the Pakistani people seize the opportunities that these successful elections now present. Requests in the 2009 base and the 2009 bridge supplemental will fund democracy and governance programs, including programs that seek to strengthen the judiciary.

In anticipation of a transition to a democratic government in Bangladesh following elections scheduled for December, our 2009 budget requests $21 million in support of democracy and governance programs, more than double the 2008 enacted level. U.S. assistance will promote comprehensive anti-corruption reforms; strengthen the government institutions, particularly at the local level; and support democratic political party development.

SUPPORTING OPPORTUNITIES AND THE FOUNDATIONS OF DEMOCRACY

While democratic institutions are extremely important, stability can really only be achieved when the basic needs of the region's most vulnerable citizens are met. Poverty is a breeding ground for political instability and the margins of society are frequently the most susceptible to extremist ideology. Our health, education and economic programs seek to improve the quality of life for the most vulnerable people. Our 2009 base request includes $283 million for health and $222 million for education in South Asia.

In India, we continue to strengthen our partnership by helping the Indians address the health needs of their most vulnerable people, including $21 million for HIV/AIDS projects in 2009. I would note that our assistance request for India has decreased slightly in Fiscal Year 2009 in recognition of the continuing growth of the Indian economy and the ability of the government to fund more of these important programs.

Education is another key component to improving quality of life and one of the most important building blocks for a vibrant economy. In Pakistan, we are requesting $117 million for basic education and $47 million for higher education in the 2009 base budget. Improving Pakistan's educational system is key to its long-term prosperity, stability and democracy and provides an alternative to extremism. Our assistance will support Pakistan's education reform in such critical areas as teacher training and improving access for girls and women. It will build schools in the Tribal Areas, provide scholarships and foster science and technology cooperation between the U.S. and Pakistan.

In addition to health and education, alleviating poverty through economic opportunity and growth is equally as important in encouraging a stable region. Our request for economic growth funding is as robust as that for health and education. Across the region we are promoting improvements to infrastructure, including roads, communications and energy solutions crucial to economic development. We are also working with governments to implement key macroeconomic reforms and adopt growth promoting trade and investment policies.

The Reconstruction Opportunity Zone legislation recently introduced to Congress would authorize President Bush to establish Reconstruction Opportunity Zones in Afghanistan and the border regions of Pakistan and would enable non-trade sensitive exports such as rugs, gemstones and handicrafts to enter the U.S. duty-free. If passed by Congress, these Zones would compel private sector investment and provide a source of employment for the Pakistan border and Afghan populations who might otherwise be targeted for terrorist recruitment.

To augment individual country assistance, we are requesting a substantial funding increase to our regional account. Our regional assistance programs seek to take advantage of synergies amongst countries to broadly promote the development of fully sovereign, stable, democratic states in South and Central Asia that are integrated into the world economy and cooperating with one another, the United States and its partners. We find that some of the most difficult issues facing our countries are indeed found across the region and can be better tackled through cooperation with neighbors.

IMPROVING SECURITY AND COUNTERTERRORISM CAPABILITY

Insurgents in Afghanistan and in Pakistan's frontier region continue to pose a serious threat to regional stability and to the safety of the United States and the rest of the world. Ensuring that Afghanistan and Pakistan have the capability to maintain their own security continues to be a primary objective. Thus, our 2009 base budget requests increased funding for programs aimed at helping governments build and sustain their own capacity for providing security to their people.

In Afghanistan, the increase will fund training for local forces in counterterrorism methods and best practices and deepen our support of Provincial Reconstruction Teams.

In Pakistan, our 2009 base request of $300 million and an additional $100 million requested in the 2009 bridge supplemental will continue to support Pakistan's security force modernization, enhance the country's counterinsurgency and counterterrorism capabilities, and provide equipment and training in support of the Security Development Plan for the Federally Administered Tribal Areas and surrounding agencies. Equipment upgrades and acquisitions will increase the capacity of Pakistan to secure its borders and fight the insurgency. This funding will also support expanding and upgrading the capabilities of the Frontier Corps to become a viable local force for securing the western border region in conjunction with the Pakistani military. Equipping and training the Pakistani military is an important part of building a strong and lasting relationship with Pakistan and recognizing their role as a regional ally.

Our counter-narcotics efforts continue to play a significant role in countering insurgency and creating stability in the region, particularly in Afghanistan where poppy cultivation fuels corruption and narcotics addiction, and is a source of financing for criminal and insurgent groups. This year we expect that about 24 provinces of 34 will be poppy free or have "low" poppy cultivation. This is a significant achievement; although overall poppy cultivation will likely remain the same or decrease slightly. Where we can properly implement our strategy, it is working. We need to redouble our efforts in southern and western Afghanistan which suffer from poor security conditions and poor governance. Our request for $313 million in the 2009 base and another $185 million in the 2009 bridge supplemental will fund our comprehensive five-pillar strategy involving public information, alternative development, law enforcement, interdiction, and eradication.

BUDGET REQUEST OVERVIEW

We have made progress on a broad range of fronts in South Asia. Particular achievements include economic growth, strengthened local and national institutions, and successes in countering insurgents. But that's not enough and important challenges remain, most prominently in the fields of counter terrorism, improving governments' capacity to provide basic services, and strengthening democratic practices and institutions.

The President's Fiscal Year 2009 base budget request for South Asian states—Afghanistan, Pakistan, Bangladesh, India, Nepal, Sri Lanka, and Maldives—is just over $2 billion dollars. Much of our request remains concentrated in Afghanistan and Pakistan, which are key to regional stability.

Ensuring the success of our security and reconstruction efforts in Afghanistan continues to be our highest priority. Accordingly, just under half of our total assistance to South Asia supports our assistance priorities in Afghanistan. Afghanistan is not just a battle theater to fight enemies, but a place of opportunity to have a close, democratic ally in the heart of a continent with considerable political and economic potential. For decades, Afghanistan has acted as a barrier between the countries of South and Central Asia. As stability in Afghanistan increases, so do the possibilities for the movement of goods, people and ideas between the countries of the region.

Our assistance and engagement in Pakistan are designed to help it develop into a stable, moderate, democratic country. Consistent with our assistance priorities, portions of our aid to Pakistan will continue to be dedicated to its western frontier, including the Federally Administered Tribal Areas. The goal is to spur development, enhance Pakistan's counter-insurgency capability, and improve coordination overall. Specifically, we aim to address the heath, education and economic programs in the Tribal Areas through the continuation of our five-year, $750 million funding commitment that began in Fiscal Year 2007. We've requested $60 million in the Fiscal Year 2008 supplemental and $150 million in the Fiscal Year 2009 base to fulfill this commitment. Building a strong, lasting partnership with Pakistan plays a pivotal role in broader counter terrorism efforts and is an important factor in our overall success in supporting a stable and prosperous Afghanistan.

DONOR COORDINATION

The United States is one of the largest donors in South Asia, if not the largest. But, we can't do it all. As assistance resources grow scarce in meeting rising needs, donor coordination is increasingly important. Since 2001, the international community has made multi-year financial pledges (through 2013) of assistance to Afghanistan totaling over $43 billion. This continuing commitment defies conventional wisdom about donor fatigue in Afghanistan. In fact, with few exceptions, most countries have proven to be reliable international partners committed to preventing Afghanistan from slipping back to its past as a sanctuary for terrorism.

The chief problem with international assistance in Afghanistan is not a shortage of funding, but the effectiveness of donor coordination. We are hopeful that the recent appointment of Special Representative of the UN Secretary-General Kai Eide and the enhanced mandate of the UN Assistance Mission in Afghanistan will improve donor coordination this year. At the Paris Support Conference in June, the international community will reaffirm our long-term commitment to Afghanistan, and raise new financial pledges to support the Afghanistan National Development Strategy and upcoming elections.

THE FOREIGN ASSISTANCE PROCESS

As with any new process, we continue to work through the new procedures and relationships, including a new foreign assistance Framework based on five assistance objectives. Now into the third year of the foreign assistance reforms, there is a much greater emphasis on the integration of foreign assistance into the strategic planning process and the alignment of budget requests with policy objectives. Accordingly, the Bureau of South and Central Asian Affairs has increased our coordination and consultation with counterparts at the U.S. Agency for International Development and other key providers of foreign assistance in the region.

Another change is the creation of the Coordinator for Reconstruction and Stabilization. The office of the Coordinator focuses on early warning, conflict prevention and conflict response in fragile and post-conflict states, as well as with the human causes and consequences of conflict. We continue to collaborate with the Coordinator's office to identify opportunities and develop effective programs within the region. Their assessment and programming skill-sets inform and bolster our efforts to provide the most effective and innovative assistance for countries at risk of conflict or destabilization.

CONCLUSION

In conclusion, Mr. Chairman, I would like to thank you for this opportunity to appear before this Committee. We continue to make every effort to be good stewards of our assistance resources, focusing them on the critical priorities that make up a considered strategy to realize our vision of a stable, prosperous and democratic South Asia.

I am happy to respond to your questions at this point. Thank you.

STATEMENT OF MR. MARK WARD, SENIOR DEPUTY ASSISTANT ADMINISTRATOR, BUREAU FOR ASIA, U.S. AGENCY FOR INTERNATIONAL DEVELOPMENT

Mr. WARD. You will forgive me for not trying to look at you, Mr. Chairman, but it is not my fault.

Mr. ACKERMAN. I have had that problem all my life.

Mr. WARD. I assume, Chairman Ackerman—all right.

Mr. ACKERMAN. Better you shouldn't look.

Mr. WARD. Better I shouldn't look. Exactly. All the other distinguished members of the committee that are behind me, thanks so much for having us here today. It is always a pleasure to come back to the subcommittee. This topic is of particular interest to me having served as the Senior Career Officer at USAID on South

Asia now for more than 4 years and having spent a significant portion of my Foreign Service career living in Pakistan.

You know, Mr. Chairman, I always read the letters from your subcommittee inviting me to testify because there are always some very good hints and suggestions about the things that I should cover, and I take those very seriously. I was particularly taken with the questions about what we are doing differently: What is different in the 2009 request, and how we are delivering our assistance differently? What sort of structures we have in place that are different.

So let me just highlight a couple of those differences. I think that the 2009 base and the 2009 supplemental request represent a good integration of all the priorities that Assistant Secretary Boucher has talked about and a real effort by USAID and all of the other agencies that are working in this region to maximize the impact of our foreign aid.

Afghanistan of course is at the top of the list. It is the central focus of our activities with Pakistan. The increases that we are requesting in 2009 are for the upcoming elections, improving local governance through the PRTs that Mr. Pence mentioned and higher education so that we can really start preparing out of work youth for jobs.

I was in Afghanistan a couple of weeks ago with our new administrator, Henrietta Fore, and was very pleased to attend Kabul's first ever jobs fair. In Pakistan, despite the significant challenges, we are starting to implement many new activities in the federally administered tribal areas, and that is the big change in our assistance strategy there.

The strategy for the FATA is twofold. First, to build the capacity of local government to provide better services to the people so that the people in the tribal areas understand that there is a government trying to serve them. Second, to deliver quick impact projects to demonstrate to those same people that their lives are getting better.

In some communities this will mean a new road, a well, an irrigation canal, but in all the communities what it will mean is people having a stake in their own future for the first time.

The 2009 request for Pakistan will also allow USAID to expand its programs in parts of the country where we have not been working before, such as the Swat Valley in the north, southern Punjab and northern Sindh, areas that have not been getting much attention from the government and the other donors, and areas where we have seen growing unrest.

In India more than 50 years of United States assistance have really paid off, with terrific gains, such that India is now a donor providing major assistance in Afghanistan and Sudan.

Our assistance levels are not going up in India, but we are providing more assistance for HIV and AIDS, at least in the 2009 request, and we are trying much more than we have in the past, and this is the real change in India, more and more to leverage private money where our goal is to leverage $4 of private donations for every 1 public dollar that we spend for assistance.

We think we have a real chance at meeting that goal in India given the vibrancy of the private sector in that country. We will continue to stay focused on the huge number of people living way below the poverty line. We think that is our responsibility as a donor, to look at those underserved segments of the population both to combat poverty, which of course is USAID's birth right, but also because it is within those communities that extremists can really profit.

Nepal, as you mentioned, is in the process of forming a new government. I was also there a couple of weeks ago and had the opportunity to talk to some of the current ministers and what they are seeing for the future. Implementation of the peace agreement and restoration of a representative government in the rural areas where the Maoists had been in control remain significant challenges.

The 2009 request is a little below the 2008 level, but we are going to be spending more of our resources on programs for youth, and democracy and governance to take advantage of the changes there and try to cement, give youth an opportunity that have been left out of so many programs while the insurgency reigned in the countryside, give them an opportunity for some job skills programs to become more employable, and obviously the importance of democracy and governance programs there as we are trying to get communities back involved in their government.

In Sri Lanka, as you said, continuing concerns there. It is a difficult environment for USAID to work in because of the security situation and because of the prohibitions on dealing with the LTTE. That is why you will find that we continue to do very little in the north. In the east, however, and in some of the poorer districts around the LTTE controlled areas in the north you are going to see more USAID programs in the future.

We are going to try to cement some of the improvements that we have seen since the east was liberated from the Tigers; that will be the key change in Sri Lanka: More of a focus on those parts of the country that we now have access to. Again, this is not an increase, but, in fact, a decrease, in part because of concerns that we have about some of the issues you mentioned and human rights abuses, but it still is a focus on the east.

In Bangladesh, again, a country in transition, where we will focus strengthening governance. This is a critical time. The overall 2009 request is above the 2008 request.

There have been some decreases in our spending for health, but that is because they are making progress on their own, there is less of a reliance on donor funding there and an appreciation on our side that we need to support some of the governance reforms that the care taker government, which you mentioned, has put in place in the last year that we hope will continue with the new elected government.

I want to spend a few minutes talking about structures and how we are delivering assistance differently in South Asia that I think will be of interest to the subcommittee. When I traveled with our administrator to Afghanistan a couple of weeks ago, I was very taken with her public remarks that we need to start Afghanizing our assistance program a lot more than we have in the past.

What that means is using local contractors in Afghanistan, and Pakistan as well, and putting incentives on international contractors, where we need to hire international contractors, to ensure that they are hiring locals as much as possible, even in key positions of management. We can do that through incentive clauses in our bid documents.

We are also trying to buy more locally in South Asia at the local and regional levels. It is more cost efficient. It also speeds up the time required to mobilize and get supplies on site, and it increases capacity of local firms that are supplying those goods and services.

We have talked before in this subcommittee about the importance of vetting. Four of the countries in South Asia now require antiterrorism certifications from our contractors and grantees to ensure that none of our money, and I wish Mr. Pence were here to hear this, none of our money is getting to the hands of organizations linked to terrorists. I know he has been concerned about that in the past.

The PRTs continue to be a very important modality for us in Afghanistan. As I said earlier, we will be increasing the funding for programs run out of the PRTs. We are putting more people in the PRTs. We are even putting some Afghan professionals that work for us now in the PRTs, which add a continuity that has been missing in the past where we have had officers rotating through after a year. Now we are going to have some real continuity.

As Mr. Pence mentioned, we are also now beginning to work with United States Special Forces in those parts of Afghanistan that are even no go for the PRTs.

We can't leave any area without development assistance and we are working effectively with the Special Forces to come up with strategies for them to go in with kinetic operations to clear an area and we know where it is coming, we know where it is going to be, and then we are able to go in there very quickly after combat operations end to hold the area with quick community development activities.

Henrietta Fore, the administrator of USAID, is very big on public/private partnerships, and she is pushing us to triple the number of public/private partnerships. South Asia has 21 active public/private partnerships today. I mentioned India. It is probably in the lead. I am pleased to say that on Monday this week Secretary Rice launched the International Women's Empowerment Fund.

It is just the latest public/private partnership fund that the administration has set up, and this one to empower women in the Muslim world in entrepreneurship, political leadership and the rule of law.

[Electronic interference.]

Mr. WARD. The new program that used to be called Section 1207 of the National Defense Authorization Act, now it is Section 1210, to expand the development impact and sustainability of our programs with Department of Defense funds, is really catching on in South Asia. The first country to apply for and successfully obtain these funds was Nepal. This year, Sri Lanka and Bangladesh have proposals in for review as well.

And my——

[Electronic interference.]

Mr. WARD [continuing]. I will talk fast. Finally, and perhaps the most important, is the Foreign Service Officer workforce. It has been steadily shrinking, and currently stands at about half of what it was in 1980 despite a significant increase in our responsibilities around the world.

The President's 2009 request for USAID's operating expenses includes significant funds for a development leadership initiative that would allow us to deploy 300 new Foreign Service Officers. I think this is particularly important because one of the criticisms that we have been getting from the Congress, and others and from some of your witnesses recently is the manner in which we conduct our contracting today.

With more Foreign Service Officers in the field we are going to have the ability to manage more, smaller contracts and grants so that we can shift away from relying so heavily on a few large contracts that only a few large U.S. companies have the resources to compete for. We will be able to work with more local contractors as well as smaller U.S. firms, which will give us more flexibility, increase competition and make more effective assistance on the ground.

Mr. Chairman, Administrator Fore has put forward a robust vision of a stronger, more flexible USAID, one that will continue to develop innovative approaches and expand its successful cooperation with the Department of State and the Department of Defense. Thanks for having me. I look forward to your questions.

[The prepared statement of Mr. Ward follows:]

PREPARED STATEMENT OF MR. MARK WARD, SENIOR DEPUTY ASSISTANT ADMINISTRATOR, BUREAU FOR ASIA, U.S. AGENCY FOR INTERNATIONAL DEVELOPMENT

Chairman Ackerman, Ranking Member Pence, other distinguished members of the committee, thank you for the invitation to participate in today's hearing. I appreciate the opportunity to share with the Subcommittee the perspective of the U.S. Agency for International Development (USAID) on U.S. assistance to countries in South Asia. I am eager to discuss our work in South Asia as I have spent a significant portion of my Foreign Service career in the region.

USAID's long-term strategy in South Asia is to strengthen the governments' abilities to provide basic human services and economic opportunity to their booming populations. More specifically, our priorities are to: support the stabilization, democratization and economic growth in Afghanistan and Pakistan; promote stability in Nepal and Sri Lanka; spur rapid job creation and deliver essential human services in India, Bangladesh and Nepal; support disaster preparedness throughout the region; and reinforce energy, trade and market reform.

The 2009 base and 2009 bridge supplemental requests represent an integration of these priorities and a coordinated effort both within USAID and with related agencies to maximize the impact of our foreign assistance.

ADDRESSING REGIONAL CHALLENGES

USAID's Asia Bureau receives a significant amount of appropriated funds for its programs in South Asia, reflecting the USG's strong commitment to the people and governments in the region. Our funding levels reflect the USG's foreign policy priorities; concentrating on Afghanistan and Pakistan—key programs for maintaining regional stability and addressing the war on terrorism. The funding request for South Asia is $1.4 billion in FY 2009 base funding and an additional $820 million in bridge supplemental funding for Afghanistan and Pakistan.

Reflecting national security priorities, *Afghanistan* remains a central focus of USAID activities, with an FY 2009 base request level of $771 million in Economic Support Funds (ESF) and Child Survival and Health (CSH), Public Law 480 non-emergency food aid, as well as an FY 2009 bridge supplemental request level of $750 million in ESF. USAID programs continue to focus on priorities such as infrastructure, sub-national governance, agriculture, including alternatives to poppy, and improving access to health and education, and the quality of both. The most significant changes to Afghanistan's FY 2009 base and supplemental requests include an increase in support for nationwide elections, an increase for improving local governance through our Provincial Reconstruction Team (PRT) program, and an increase for higher education so we can help prepare out-of-work youth for the job market.

We face a number of challenges in *Pakistan*, especially on the border region with Afghanistan. Despite significant challenges, USAID has started implementing many new activities in the Federally Administered Tribal Areas (FATA) in maternal and child health, education, job creation, and good governance. Our strategy for FATA is twofold. First, it focuses on building the capacity of the local government structures so that they can provide better services to the people. Second, we also have projects to demonstrate to the residents of FATA that their lives are getting better—depending on the priority needs identified by the people. In some communities this will mean a new road, a well or an irrigation canal. In all communities, this will mean people having a stake in their future development for the first time.

The FY 2009 base request of $481 million in CSH and ESF, and the FY 2009 Supplemental request of $70 million will allow USAID to expand programs in areas where we have not operated in recent years, such as the Swat Valley in the North of Pakistan. The overall FY 2009 request for Pakistan includes $150 million for the tribal areas, the third year in a five year $750 million initiative, to complement the Pakistani contribution of $1 billion over nine years towards the total $2 billion FATA Sustainable Development Plan.

In *India*, more than 50 years of U.S. assistance has helped India make tremendous gains. India has also emerged as a donor country, for Afghanistan and Sudan. USAID is working with the government, the private sector and other donors to leverage approximately five dollars for every dollar of U.S. assistance. For example, QUEST has leveraged almost $3 million in cash and in-kind contributions to link learning with livelihoods for India's youth. Through such alliances, the United States and India are committed to working in partnership to reach India's development goal of halving poverty by 2015. USAID will also focus on the poorest and most underserved segments of the population in order to combat poverty and the conditions that promote extremism.

The FY 2009 request of $74 million is lower than FY 2008 level. USAID is phasing out programs in which India has achieved significant capacity and where the private sector can contribute, such as economic growth and education, while continuing programs meeting serious social needs, such as maternal-child health.

Nepal is in the process of forming a new government. However, implementation of the peace agreement and restoration of representative government in rural areas remain significant challenges. Sustainable peace and lasting democracy also hinge on economic and social recovery in the countryside. Economic opportunities and local government services need to be expanded in order to restore public faith in government.

The USG is waiting to see how the new government forms before committing to a strategy of engagement with it. We would like to work with other donors to support Nepal's transition to peace, build a strong and representative government, establish the rule of law, end human rights abuses and address social inequality and poverty. The FY 2009 request of $12 million is less than the FY 2008 level. However, several strategic shifts have occurred to best position us to support the peace process. This will mean a relative shift in focus from health in favor of efforts to create greater economic opportunity for the poor, particularly youth, as well as a significant increase for democracy and governance activities.

In *Sri Lanka*, the USG remains committed to bilateral assistance despite the escalating conflict and deteriorating security situation. Given these realities, USAID has reassessed its priorities and has developed a new strategy to deliver assistance to the conflict-affected population.

More than before, programs will focus on regional needs while also working at a national level on some of the most critical democracy, governance and conflict mitigation issues. The new economic growth/workforce development and democracy/governance programs will address economic disparities by expanding economic and democracy-building activity in the conflict-affected East Province as well as the poorest districts on the border with the North Province, the current theater of military conflict.

USAID's FY 2009 request of $4 million for Sri Lanka is $1.2 million lower than the enacted FY 2008 level. The decrease is due in part to the completion of several tsunami reconstruction programs, and also signals our concern with human rights abuses in the country.

Bangladesh's FY 2009 budget request realigns resources to best promote peace and security by strengthening democratic governance and tackling the underlying social, demographic and economic factors that make Bangladesh vulnerable to violent extremism. The request also places resources where the United States has a comparative advantage over other donors or meets an otherwise urgent and unfunded need, particularly with respect to democracy and governance, health, education, disaster management, food security, and economic growth.

The overall FY 2009 request of $100.6 million is an increase over the FY 2008 $97 million base level. A decrease in maternal and child health needs created an opportunity to reduce CSH funds by about $7 million and increase funding for further good governance reforms that build upon positive steps taken by Bangladesh's 2007 caretaker government.

DOING BUSINESS DIFFERENTLY

In South Asia, USAID is adapting to a new style of doing business. There are several examples. USAID is committed to continually increasing the use of local contractors in all of our missions, but most importantly in Afghanistan and Pakistan. During her recent visit to Afghanistan, our new Administrator stressed the importance of more "Afghanization." We have established incentives for contractors financed by the United States to increase the use of Afghans in key personnel positions, as a means of ensuring a better understanding of the needs and reality on the ground, improving senior management capabilities in Afghanistan and controlling costs.

USAID is also looking to buy locally. We will purchase more at the local and regional levels, thereby targeting cost-efficient and quality supplies, speeding up the time it takes to mobilize on-site and increasing the capacity of local firms to deliver goods and services.

In order to help ensure that no U.S. taxpayer dollars find their way into the hands of organizations linked to terrorists, our missions in Afghanistan, Pakistan, India, and Sri Lanka have required anti-terrorism certification from all our contractors and grantees.

As you know, the security paradigm in South Asia has presented USAID with a new set of challenges in which we are constantly learning how to adapt and do business in insecure places.

The Provincial Reconstruction Teams (PRTs) in Afghanistan have provided a platform for USAID officers to monitor assistance outside of Kabul and the ability to meet regularly with local leaders. Additionally, we have recognized that there are places that even the PRTs cannot access. To overcome this challenge, USAID has assigned officers to work with the U.S. Special Forces in areas that are outside the PRTs' reach—which are either very insecure or are areas that have recently been "cleared" (i.e., post combat). In these situations, the military and USAID sit together to lay out a strategic plan for clearing an area with combat operations and then holding the area by undertaking community development activities as soon as combat ends.

Expanding the use of public-private partnerships is a top priority in today's USAID. Our new Administrator challenged us to triple the resources we leverage through public-private partnerships. Today, there are 21 active public-private alliances in South Asia, including programs in IT curriculum, strengthening universities and the garment industry, small business sector promotion and coffee and tea production. And, just this past Monday, Secretary Rice announced the International Women's Empowerment Fund, a new public-private partnership to empower women in the Muslim world in entrepreneurship, political leadership, and the rule of law.

USAID's implementation of DOD funds transferred under section 1207 of the National Defense Authorization Act (section 1210) will dramatically expand the development impact and sustainability of its programs in South Asia. These funds allow the USG to address root causes of conflict and instability in a country to reduce the need for military intervention.

Nepal was the first country to apply for, and successfully obtain, funding from the 1210 account under the FY 2007 appropriation. The process for applying for these funds continues to be refined and South Asia countries currently submitting applications include Sri Lanka and Bangladesh.

RESPONDING TO WORKFORCE CHALLENGES

Over the past several decades USAID's permanent Foreign Service Officer (FSO) workforce, has been steadily shrinking and currently stands at about half the level it did in 1980—despite a significant increase in USAID responsibilities. The President's 2009 request for USAID operating expenses includes $92.1 million for a "Development Leadership Initiative" that will allow USAID to recruit, hire and train 300 new FSOs.

This initiative will allow USAID to strengthen its technical assistance experts and seize the opportunities presented for development around the world. More specifically, it is my hope that a side effect of increasing our workforce will be that USAID is better equipped to manage smaller, country-specific contracts and grants and we can shift away from the large contracts that are often awarded to a small group of U.S.-based companies. With an increased workforce, we can work with more local contractors as well as smaller U.S.-based firms. This will provide more flexibility, increased competition, and more effective assistance on the ground, where it matters.

CONCLUSION

In Asia, USAID recognizes that the stakes for development and foreign assistance have never been higher. Administrator Fore has put forward a robust vision of a stronger, more flexible Agency—one that will be able to continue to develop innovative approaches and that will be able to expand its successful cooperation with the Departments of State and Defense. We look forward to working together with the Congress in the year ahead to ensure that we maximize the impact of the generous foreign assistance provided by the American people.

Mr. Chairman, thank you for the opportunity to appear before you and Members of the Committee today. I am happy to take any questions you may have.

Mr. ACKERMAN. Thank both of you for your excellent statements. The first question that I would like to pose is framed in the irony of coming from a subcommittee chairman of a full committee that spent countless thousands of dollars upgrading our equipment and can't tell you how the heck we spent it.

So the first question, with that caveat, last week we had both Ambassadors Holbrook and Pickering before our full committee to discuss Pakistan. One of the points that they each made struck me. They both very strongly asserted that the majority of the money Congress provides for assistance in both Pakistan and Afghanistan doesn't reach the Pakistani or Afghan people.

They testified that the money disappears into consulting fees, overhead costs, and much of it never even leaves the United States. Can each or either of you tell us what percentage of the assistance Congress provides for either nation actually reaches its intended recipients?

For the record, we are currently advised by our technical people that much of the amplifying system that is in the individual microphones, including the witness table, are defective and are going to have to be replaced. We are not going to do that today. So if we can hear from our internally displaced witnesses?

Mr. WARD. Very good question. I am delighted you asked it. In anticipation of that question, I mentioned in my opening remarks about the efforts that we are making to increase our rank so that we can do more local contracting and insert clauses in our bid documents to make clear to the bidding community out there that we want to be hiring more locally.

When Ambassador Pickering, who I was honored to serve under in Moscow, and Ambassador Holbrook made these points, I would question the use of the word waste or that the money is not getting to the people. Buying top technical assistance is expensive, and in a country like Afghanistan where they have been at war for 25 years, that capacity did not exist in country when we first went back in at the end of 2001, the beginning of 2002.

I accept, and I know Assistant Secretary Boucher agrees with me because we have had this conversation before, that we need to be doing more to insist that more of our contracts and grants are awarded to organizations in Pakistan and in Afghanistan. Not just because too much of the money otherwise is spent on overhead back here in the United States, but also because, I would assert, we get better services.

Those are people that know those countries. It was a challenge for us to do that in Afghanistan in the early days because, as I mentioned, 25 years of fighting left them with very limited to non-existent technical capacity. It is getting better. I don't think we should change our approach overnight. There are still some sectors where the best expertise that is available is in the United States, and we should continue to have the flexibility to hire it when we need it.

There is also a lot that can be done, particularly in infrastructure, by local firms or firms in the region that don't have to mobilize from, say, the east coast of the United States, that might mobilize from a neighboring country.

Mr. ACKERMAN. It is strange that it has taken us all this time and billions of dollars to figure out that the money to be spent on the ground should be spent on the ground. How much of the funds are we talking about that were skimmed in the United States before it ever got to Afghanistan, or Pakistan, or anywhere else?

Mr. WARD. I don't think——

Mr. ACKERMAN. You can change the word skimmed.

Mr. WARD. Yes. Again, I would assert that these are costs that the United States Government was well aware of before it entered into these contracts and grants.

Mr. ACKERMAN. Could you explain, give us an example of how that happens? I know in Homeland Security when we were hiring people to be the screeners at the airport we awarded a contract to a company that immediately sold the contract to another security company after taking 20 percent off the top.

That happened three times before the actual people doing the work, which resulted in about 40 percent of the money spent on screeners, ever went to a company that actually did screening. People just milked it. That goes with the skim.

Mr. WARD. That is not our case. The complaint about the USAID funded contractors and grantees is that too much of the money that could be spent, say building a school or doing teacher training programs, is instead spent on salaries of very qualified experts and the overhead that their home offices in the United States or a European country add as part of the contract costs to support——

Mr. ACKERMAN. I am trying to get, because I am just a simple kid from Brooklyn, an easy picture of what this looks like.

Mr. BOUCHER. Mark, can I try?

Mr. WARD. Sure.

Mr. ACKERMAN. I mean, I know that good, qualified people when they were told that we needed a hammer, you know, had meetings and decided what a hammer looked like, and they sat around designing hammers, and we spent lots of money designing hammers and came out with something that looked like a hammer, and it cost, you know, $300, $700, $2,000 toilet, whatever it was, that, you know, someone could have just gone down to Lowe's, or Home Depot, or somebody and said, hey, that is it.

When we are doing schools are we saying to somebody, what should a school look like? Can you draw a picture? Can you get an architect?

Mr. BOUCHER. No. Perhaps I can explain it this way.

Mr. ACKERMAN. We are talking about lots of money.

Mr. BOUCHER. Lots of money, but there is a factor here. AID has lost people over the last few years. They don't have as many direct contracting officers. People who can go out in the field can negotiate contracts, sign them and supervise them.

Mr. ACKERMAN. They lost a lot of people because they go to the other side?

Mr. BOUCHER. No. They lost a lot of people because over the last 10, 15 years they have been cut, cut, cut, right? Vietnam, there were——

[Electronic interference.]

Mr. BOUCHER [continuing]. People in the field to administer or organize big contracts, to handle a lot of direct contracting. We are trying to increase that. We are actually underway now at——

Mr. ACKERMAN. But how much money or what is the percentage that stays in the United States before it actually hits the ground?

Mr. BOUCHER. It depends on the contract. If you go down to the lower levels you will see——

Mr. ACKERMAN. Give me an overall picture. Half?

Mr. BOUCHER. No.

Mr. WARD. I used to actually be the head of procurement for USAID so I have been asked this question a lot, and all you can do is a sort of mean. Every organization has a U.S. Government-approved overhead rate that it uses for our contracting. I think that on the high end it might touch 30 percent. For some of the not-for-profits, their overhead is going to be much closer to, say, 10 percent.

Even if we hired an Afghan firm or a firm in the neighborhood——

Mr. ACKERMAN. So not-for-profits do it for a third of what we can do?

Mr. WARD. Well, not-for-profits have a lot less overhead.

Mr. ACKERMAN. Government's making a bigger profit than the not-for-profits? Three to one?

Mr. WARD. No. I am comparing a for profit firm that would, say, do infrastructure with an organization, a not-for-profit, that might, say, do community development activities or training activities at the local level. Their overhead rates, you know, their cost of doing business that gets passed on to the government——

Mr. ACKERMAN. I don't understand why. Forgive me for dwelling on this one question, but to me, that is the——

Mr. BOUCHER. It is a serious question, and, as Mark indicated——

Mr. ACKERMAN. Every time we need to build a sewer somewhere we have to decide, we have to have overhead to figure out how to build a sewer, and if we move it from one country to another it is more overhead?

Mr. BOUCHER. No. I will give you an example. Mr. Pence referred to the fact he was in Kunar province. Kunar province, they built a road up the river based on the expertise that they had in the provincial reconstruction team and in the governor's office there. They had enough expertise, and project management and stuff to build that road by and large. They employed some experts from outside.

There are now engaged in building the bridges, 16 bridges, across this river that he referred to that he saw. When I went to the PRTs I said, how are you doing that? The answer is they have to go to Kabul and get bigger contracts and more engineering skills because the bridges require higher levels of expertise.

If you then take that another step up, another step up, you get to the point where you have big projects that require sophisticated project management, which doesn't yet exist in Afghanistan. So what we have to do, and Mr. Ward and I have been working on this, is to get more and more qualified Afghan contractors, get more and more people out there——

Mr. ACKERMAN. What ever happened to those guys from the Bridge on the River Kwai? I mean, you know, before the movie was over they had a bridge.

Mr. BOUCHER. I know. It is not the same kind of bridge.

Mr. WARD. And that is another point that Ambassador Boucher closed with. You know, the notion that the United States Government should do it on the cheap, we don't——

Mr. ACKERMAN. God forbid.

Mr. WARD. No, but there is an important point. You know, October 2005 when the earthquake hit northern Pakistan, children that were killed on that Saturday morning were in school. The United States Government built schools in Afghanistan and Pakistan, and we will not build to any standard that will, you know, fall in an earthquake. That is more expensive.

That is going to require an expertise that will probably bring with it some overhead. I think what we just have to do is balance that. In an area where we need additional engineering expertise we should look at bringing in an expatriate firm.

Mr. ACKERMAN. Schools are built to earthquake proof standards?

Mr. WARD. Yes, in those areas where earthquakes are prevalent. In fact, one of the fascinating things we are doing in northern Pakistan right now is bringing parents down to see the blueprints of the schools and to see the construction underway because, frankly, parents are afraid of schools right now because of what happened on that Saturday morning.

So we are trying to get parents to be confident about sending their kids back to school again by showing them all the rebar, I don't understand it all, but all the material that goes into the construction. We have one of the top engineering firms in the United States there supporting the construction that is being done by a Pakistani firm.

I think because of the earthquake challenge you do need some foreign expertise in there, and it is going to be expensive. I think sometimes we have to do that. I think what Assistant Secretary Boucher and I are trying to do is not have a sort of one size fits all where you don't always have to have all that expensive expertise.

Mr. ACKERMAN. When an earthquake hits another country, do we start all over again and try to figure out how to build an earthquake proof school, and have new people design it and go through that process all over again? Do we go to the earthquake proof school folder, and pull it out, and say here is an earthquake proof school plan, why don't we just implement it?

Mr. WARD. It depends on the capacity in that government to build schools. I mean, Pakistan's earthquake standards are fine on paper. The issue is, Are they in fact enforcing them when they build their own schools? The answer we saw on that Saturday morning.

Mr. BOUCHER. But I have to say, sir, we do have standard designs. The 65 schools we are building in the tribal areas, I visited one of them, and they are built on a standard design that was developed with expertise from the United States and Pakistan. Pakistani firms know how to build them, and so that is what they are building in the tribal areas. It is a good design, and we use it.

Once we have got it we can use it again and again, but sometimes when you are going into an area or you are going back to an earthquake area, you have to do some redesign.

Mr. ACKERMAN. Is there an existing Federal schedule that says this is the reimbursement rate? Contractors who are building a school in degree of difficulty country A, you will be reimbursed $20,000 per floor. Like when I call up my health insurance company and they tell me you got Sickness No. 7, you are only getting $32 regardless of how much you think it is going to cost.

Then my doctor, if he wants to accept the contract, takes $37 or whatever it is.

Mr. WARD. No is the answer to your question.

Mr. ACKERMAN. I thought I would never say this, but we need the health insurance industry to come in and give us some guidance because they know how to keep the costs under control to make a profit. If we are the company that is looking to save money, you know, USA Incorporated, we should know what a school is going to, you know, roughly.

Mr. WARD. Mr. Chairman, I think what is supposed to happen is the competition between these companies——

Mr. ACKERMAN. What competition?

Mr. WARD. There are big companies that bid on these jobs, and competition between them is supposed to help keep the costs in line.

Mr. ACKERMAN. Do they really compete?

Mr. WARD. Yes, absolutely.

Mr. ACKERMAN. How much profit do they make on $1 million?

Mr. WARD. One would need to ask them. I think they hold that pretty close.

Mr. ACKERMAN. Yes, I know, but we should have an idea because if my doctor was charging $7 million for whooping cough, my insurance company wouldn't pay it. There are a lot of doctors competing out there.

Mr. WARD. Remember, we are talking about working in Afghanistan and Pakistan, very difficult areas where there is also cost for security. In answer to your question, each of these firms is audited by a Federal agency which approved their overhead rate. Now, that is an overhead rate for all countries. It is not per country, it is not based on what they do.

Again, competition is supposed to help, but the reason that Assistant Secretary Boucher and I have been pushing to get more firms involved and the reason why I am so pleased that Administrator Fore is with us on this is that we can enlarge the pool of firms that are going to bid on these jobs if we break them down, if we have more officers who can manage more, smaller contracts, not these mega contracts like we have had to use in the past when we had so few officers that is all we can keep an eye on.

If we have more officers to keep an eye on a bigger number of smaller contracts, that means there are a lot of firms out there, particularly in the area in which we are working, Afghanistan, Pakistan, that can compete. They can't compete now. If we go out on the street with a bid document for a $100 million construction project, there are very few firms that can compete, there are probably no firms in Afghanistan that can compete for that.

There are a couple in Pakistan that could. We need to break those down so that we don't have mega contracts. One way to do that, and that is why we have been talking about it, is to get more officers out there such as we used to have so that we have more people to keep an eye on smaller activities.

We hear you, and we support it and welcome these questions because this is a big shift for us.

Mr. ACKERMAN. Secretary Boucher, in your statement you discuss supporting Afghanistan's local officials and supporting their efforts to reach their people. How does assistance do that, and how do the Afghan people know?

Mr. BOUCHER. It does it in a variety of ways, sir. One of the better things that is happening this year in Afghanistan is more Afghan ownership at the local level. They have been appointing good officials at the provincial level and the lower sub governor level, the district level.

What we are doing this year is we are putting some of our money into pots that those people can start using to finance projects. They have all engaged in discussions with the local population. There are provincial development plans in each of the provinces now that have been done through consultation with the local population. We are trying to put money in the hands of capable people who can do those things.

The PRTs do projects locally in consultation with the governors and the local people. A lot of things like the, what do you call it, good performance initiative, the good performance fund for antinarcotics where if a governor is able to reduce and eradicate poppy in his region he can apply for some of these funds.

I was just up in the north in Mazari Sharif, and they got their first shipment of tractors under that money. So I think as Afghanistan generally starts to build these capabilities to do governance at the local level, we have tried to push more money out there. Mr. Ward has recently I think changed the rules for his people at PRTs so that they can spend larger amounts of money directly in consultation with local governors.

Mr. ACKERMAN. In your statement you tell us that the administration is attempting to strengthen Pakistan's judiciary. How does that happen when one of our coalition partners has withdrawn its ministers from the cabinet in a dispute over restoring the judiciary?

Mr. BOUCHER. It is something we want to do, it is something we are going to do, but they have to solve the political problems first.

So at this point we are looking to them to resolve this political issue of restoration of judges; however they decide to do it.

I have made clear to the leaders of the major parties, as Deputy Secretary Negroponte made clear to the prime minister, that we want to support an independent judiciary in Pakistan. We have had I think some programs in this area already, but in terms of doing a major push in this area it will be once they solve the political questions involving the judiciary.

We have been strongly supportive as well of other institutions, like the election commission. I think one of the areas where we will be able to do a lot more with the new government is to help build and strengthen democratic institutions.

Mr. ACKERMAN. Did we give them a timeframe in which to do that?

Mr. BOUCHER. No, it is up to them to decide how they are going to solve this issue, and, as you noted, it has gotten pretty political between the parties and they are just going to have to figure it out.

Mr. ACKERMAN. So we could be waiting a long time?

Mr. BOUCHER. Conceivably. I think, you know, they are at an impasse right now, but that doesn't make it permanent. So we will just have to see how things evolve. There are other institutions I think that we can readily work with, including, you know, more local levels of the justice system, and police and things like that.

Mr. ACKERMAN. Thank you. Mr. Ward, in your statement you note the emergence of the Maoists as part of the government in Nepal. To quote you, you say, "the USG is waiting to see how the new government forms before committing to a strategy of engagement with it." Does that mean that you anticipate the Maoists may not be a part of the government so United States assistance can continue to be provided to Nepal, and what do we do if the Maoists are in the government?

Mr. WARD. The current rules which we operate under, a license from the Office of Foreign Assets Control, allows us to deal with members of government that happen to be from the Maoist party. This was a result of the peace agreement that was signed in 2006.

Mr. BOUCHER. Yes.

Mr. WARD. As of today, we are continuing to do everything that we were doing in Nepal before the most recent elections.

When I say that we need to do assessments to decide what our engagements with the government are going to look like in the future it is not because we anticipate or would even speculate about who will be in the government and who will not, but it is really more to look at opportunities that we see to engage in sectors that we were not able to engage in very effectively before because so much of the country just wasn't available for our programs for security reasons and because of our disinterest in working in areas that were governed by the Maoists.

So I am sorry if I gave you that impression in that language. It is more that we want to assess the right mix of activities, such as which sectors we can be most effective in when we hear from the new government what its priorities are going to be, and when we hear from the other donors what their priorities are going to be.

Mr. BOUCHER. Sir, if I can just say, there are some policy issues raised by the Maoists coming into government and probably leading the government. The designations of the Maoists are under two separate terrorism designations. One is a specially designated global terrorist list and the other is a terrorist exclusion list.

Those don't automatically prohibit any assistance to ministries or other entities that would be controlled by the Maoists, but we have a policy issue here. We have been engaged in a process for the last year to try to get the Maoists to abandon violence and adopt politics, adopt a peaceful practice and enter into politics.

To the extent that they do that, that they do both, abandon violence and engage in politics, we will be able to work with them more. I note, for example, some of the other major parties have called on the Maoists to disband the young communist league, which has been reported to be involved in a lot of the sort of thugishness and violence that still exists in the countryside, to either disband it or fundamentally transform it.

That kind of step would be the kind of step we would look for, too, in terms of seeing the Maoists embrace a peaceful and political path. To the extent that they take such steps, we can have a better relationship with them.

Our Ambassador has met with the Prachanda, the Maoist leader, and basically told him that, that we will work with a peaceful government, we will work with a government that is committed to democracy, but to the extent to which we can work with you, and your ministers and your people is going to depend on the extent to which you abandon violence and embrace politics.

Mr. ACKERMAN. There is a similar situation in Sri Lanka where the TMVP, which as I pointed out although not a designated terrorist organization is a splinter of the LTTE, is now a part of the provincial government. How is that circumstance going to affect our programs in the east provinces?

Mr. BOUCHER. It is also a policy question that we are looking at. I think first and foremost, our emphasis right now is trying to get the militant group that is associated with the TMVP, the so-called Palian faction, to get them to end their use of child soldiers. That is a matter of congressional legislation; it is a matter of great importance to us.

I think UNICEF has estimated there is something like 150 child soldiers in this group plus or minus. I don't know. It is probably a vague estimate. A couple dozen have been released so far. We are engaged in a concerted effort of trying to get the government to help us to make sure that these child soldiers are no longer members of this group.

We will look at operate in the east. We have wanted to try to make sure that the people of this region who have been subject to fighting, and displacement and a lot of other troubles over the last few years, we want to try to help them stabilize and help them enjoy the benefits of living under a democratic government and living in a new situation.

How exactly we do that and run these programs will depend to some extent on how this new elected government operates and whether the associated groups end their violent activities.

Mr. ACKERMAN. Thank you. Mr. Ward, in your opening remarks you stated that we are continuing the HIV/AIDS money with respect to India and are going to increase it. We have been trying to verify that because in your Fiscal Year 2009 congressional budget justification, which I have here, on page 607 where you have India and you have the chart, it shows that in 2009 under the line of Global HIV/AIDS Initiative, you have zeroed it out.

If we go to the regional south central Asia on page 644, again, Fiscal Year 2009, you have zeroed it out. How does that represent an increase or is there something else you are doing that is not in the budget?

Mr. WARD. It is complicated. The figures that I have been given I can share with you. I think what might be more useful to the subcommittee is if we get back to you with a fuller explanation. There are a lot of different accounts.

Mr. ACKERMAN. Yes. It is complicated is a pretty skimpy explanation.

Mr. WARD. The numbers that I have shown in the 2009 request, the assistance for HIV and AIDS, which is not just coming out of that global account but also out of our child survival and health account, is going up over what the base was in 2008.

Mr. ACKERMAN. So whatever the number for the child survival account, it is really going to be less because some of that money should be in the HIV/AIDS account?

Mr. WARD. For reasons I don't understand, and which is why I would like to get back to the——

Mr. ACKERMAN. Are we stealing from Paulita to pay Paul?

Mr. WARD [continuing]. The global HIV/AIDS money for India is not showing up in the CBJ. I don't understand that, and that is what we need to get back to you and explain.

Mr. ACKERMAN. Yes, because when you understand it, could you explain it to us?

Mr. WARD. Yes, yes.

Mr. ACKERMAN. We are most anxious to hear how it represents an increase if we don't see any dollars.

Mr. WARD. But you are absolutely right to ask the question. I mean, there are more than 2.5 million people infected with HIV in India, and this is exactly one of the groups that we should stay committed to.

Mr. ACKERMAN. And the President has so stated we are committed to it.

Mr. WARD. Yes.

Mr. ACKERMAN. But wishing it were so, and hoping it were so and praying it were so doesn't put any money in the program. So until we see the money in the program, it ain't so.

Mr. WARD. I will get back to you very shortly with an answer, and I hope it is a clear answer.

[The information referred to follows:]

WRITTEN RESPONSE RECEIVED FROM MR. MARK WARD TO QUESTION ASKED DURING THE HEARING BY THE HONORABLE GARY L. ACKERMAN

The President's FY 2009 request for health assistance in India is $73.565m.

Of this amount, the President is requesting $21m for HIV/AIDS from the Child Survival and Health (CSH) account. This is a slight increase over the FY 2008 actual level.

India has also been the recipient of funding as a 'non-focus country' for the Global HIV/AIDS Initiative (GHAI) account since 2005.

India received $6M in GHAI funding in FY 2008 and we anticipate they will receive similar funding in FY 2009. However, "non-focus" GHAI country resources are not allocated until the year of implementation. Thus no amount appears in the FY2009 CBJ for India under GHAI.

We will report back to you when we know the GHAI allocation for India for FY 2009.

Mr. ACKERMAN. I look forward to it. Where do we go from here? Back to Ambassador Boucher. We note that your statement discusses the question of effectiveness of donor coordination, and you cite the recent appointment of the Special Representative of the U.N. Secretary General as helping to improve donor coordination.

The question is, Is Afghanistan not important enough to United States security that we shouldn't rely on others to ensure that there is coordination between donors? Shouldn't we make sure of that ourselves?

Mr. BOUCHER. Sir, I think we do spend a lot of time on better coordination within the U.S. Government, within all our agencies, but also within the international community. A lot of my time on the road is spent as it was last week in Paris working with the French on the upcoming donors' conference, working with Kai Eide, the U.N. representative who is the new special representative, on coordination to make sure we are focused on the same goals, and we are focused on the same practices as we all work to support the Afghan Government.

In terms of sort of assuming that overall leadership, we do think the United Nations is the best place to do it. United States, as the biggest donor, has a very important role. We do coordinate, for example, on police training where others have roles in police training, but our general at the combined command Alpha in Afghanistan does, in fact, pretty much coordinate with everybody on doing that.

There are other areas, broadly civilian reconstruction, where we all look to the United Nations to give us guidance and lead and to be the primary coordinator for support for the Afghan Government.

Mr. WARD. If I can just add to that. A couple of weeks ago on this trip I keep referring to that our administrator took to Afghanistan and Pakistan, she led a group of I think two dozen other donor countries to a 1-day conference in Kabul where Kai Eide appeared, the Government of Afghanistan obviously was chairing the meeting, to discuss just that, Mr. Chairman, how the U.N. and all of the donors can better coordinate in a lead up discussion to the Paris conference that Assistant Secretary Boucher referred to.

So I think it is absolutely right that the United Nations and the Government of Afghanistan need to be in the lead, but the United States, among the donors, is very much in the lead on donor coordination.

Mr. ACKERMAN. Thank you for that. Mr. Secretary, your statement talks about assistance to Bangladesh in anticipation of a transition to a democratic government. Shouldn't we be providing assistance to ensure that elections are free and fair and that the government that emerges is democratic as well as legitimate? Is that a softball?

Mr. BOUCHER. The answer is absolutely, sir. If you look from 2008 to 2009, support for democratic institution, we have asked for going from $9 million to $20 million. A lot of that is to be able to support the elections. We have been a very strong supporter of the independent election commission in Bangladesh.

We are just starting a program to work over next I think it is 3 or 4 years on anticorruption efforts. Others are doing the anticorruption commission, we are working on the government budget and how it is spent to try to prevent corruption. We have made a big point in our talk and our finance of strengthening the institutions that can help preserve and protect democracy, and I think we are indeed putting our money where our mouth is on that one.

In addition, on a policy level we have been pressing for the steps that we think are necessary in order to provide a good election, to provide a good playing field for the parties to contest the election.

I made the point quite vocally when I was in Bangladesh that the state of emergency needs to be lifted, and indeed, a couple of days later the chief advisor, who I think had been preparing to say this anyway, but he started talking about lifting the ban on indoor political activity and some other steps.

I do think they got the message quite clearly that you can't have a good election under a state of emergency. So it is both working with them and pressing the policy points, but also trying to put money into the election commission, the anticorruption efforts, civil service commissions and the other institutions that can hold good elections and guarantee stability for the democracy.

Mr. WARD. If I can just take this opportunity while we are on Bangladesh to also make a plug for, and it is in the administration's request, funding to continue for disaster preparedness.

I will never forget my visits to the area that was hit by Cyclone Sidar a couple of months after it happened to see what the earthen dams that they had put in with our assistance over the years and the mangrove swamps looked like after the cyclone hit them. They looked terrible, but they looked terrible because they did their job. The communities behind those earthen dams and the communities behind those mangrove swamps were in pretty good shape.

The numbers of fatalities after that cyclone were, I mean you hate to say this, but they were good numbers for a cyclone in Bangladesh. We need to stay. All of the things that Assistant Secretary Boucher talked about are of course terribly important on the governance side, but we also need to continue to help the Bangladesh Government because of some of the lessons we have learned from its neighbors in recent weeks in preparing for the next natural disaster.

Mr. ACKERMAN. In your statement, Mr. Ward, you note that the Government of Pakistan has committed $1 billion of its own money for development of the FATA to be used in conjunction with the assistance that we are providing for the area. Has the Government of Pakistan actually provided any of that funding that it committed?

Mr. WARD. This is a multiyear commitment, and they are on track for the first year. This is a new initiative, and we ask this question a lot, and, yes, we are off to a good start.

Mr. ACKERMAN. But what does on track mean? They recommitted?

Mr. WARD. I am sorry?

Mr. ACKERMAN. Does on track mean they recommitted?